WILD ROSE

B. EUGENE B.

WILD ROSE

& OTHER POEMS SUNG BY THE WINDOW

Be! Eugene Be! Creative

CONTENTS

Words of Praise
ix
Dedication
xi

1 — Wild Rose: An Ode to Jane Marie
2

2 — Mother Moon - Remix
8

3 — Crossing Over & Back Again
10

4 — Suspicions
12

5 — Scathing Inquiry
14

6 — A Silent Prayer in the Night
16

7 — Resilient
18

8 — A Thimble Full of Seeds
20

CONTENTS

9 — Death of Art | Art of Death
22

10 — Ashes
26

11 — What it Means to Mourn
28

12 — Mom's Eyes
30

13 — Perhaps Tomorrow
32

14 — Morning in the Mountains
34

15 — Closure
36

16 — The Last Days On Earth
38

17 — Death Watch
40

18 — Say a Little Prayer
42

19 — The World We Know is Not Real
46

20 — Collecting Rocks
48

21 — Chased by Changing Winds
50

CONTENTS

22 — Window Dressing
52

23 — Desert Mirage
54

24 — New Clothes
56

25 — Secret Places in the Forest
58

26 — One for the Road
60

27 — Dense Headspace
62

28 — Buoyancy Reserved from a Past Life
64

29 — Fire
66

30 — Air
68

31 — Water
70

32 — Overture
72

33 — Movement
74

34 — A Gasping
76

CONTENTS

35 — Soup
78

36 — Mother-Mom-Mommy-Momma
80

37 — A Gathering (Under the Sun)
82

38 — Songs of Beuren (oh! I got money problems)
84

39 — Derby Days
86

40 — The Reign of the Octopus Queen
88

41 — The Moon Carries Me Tonight
90

42 — About the Poems Contained Herein
93

43 — About: Wild Rose
94

44 — About: Other Poems Sung by the Window
97

45 — Afterword
101

About The Author
103

WORDS OF PRAISE

B. Eugene B. presents his *Wild Rose* poems as a meditation on the pain of loss. They can be read as an elegy to his beloved mother, Jane Marie—a way to keep her alive in some sense—and they can also be seen as a tender manual for grieving. The reader may be reminded that in acute grief, a certain urgent remembering compels a stockpiling of memories as a guard against forgetting. The sense that grief will fade—How could it!?—can be as terrifying as the loss itself, even as one longs for reprieve, or "a softening of the pain," as in B.'s "Closure." In these poems, B. seems to write less against losing the fine detail of his life with his mother and more to preserve the memory of how deeply he feels her loss.

B.'s mother's influence, her artistic impulses, her language, her own poems sung by the window, seem to have imprinted B. with a constellation of images—celestial, botanical, elemental—within which this entire collection revolves. In that way, the grieving tribute B. crafts here, and to which he adds his *"Other Poems,"* is an affirmation of Jane Marie's singular shape and movement within her family, and beyond.

In language that is by turns pleading, mournful, tender, wonder-filled and resolute, B.'s poetics move from the tops of bureaus to the mountains to the heavens to sacred texts to the inner worlds of both himself and his late mother. The broad reach of his grief seems to leave him with this stirring conclusion in "Death Watch": "Death is forever becoming / Coming from a place up God's immeasurable sleeve."

Kristy Gledhill, MFA

Copyright © 2023 by B. Eugene B.

All rights reserved. No part of this book may be reproduced in any manner whatsoever without written permission except in the case of brief quotations embodied in critical articles and reviews.

First Printing, 2023

To my Mom, Jane Marie. A lasting memory.

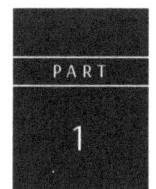

WILD ROSE

WILD ROSE: AN ODE TO JANE MARIE

WILD ROSE

III
It was she
A wild rose
[Her reliquary]

A shadow box,
With mementos from walks,
Were among other treasures she kept.

Things that were dear to her,
Remnants of memories would stir,
Like dreams as she slept.

Sticks, rocks, & thread,
A rusted key,
Keepsakes impart.

Stone arrowhead,
Small shards of pottery,
Things that were dear to her heart.

To see your smile, or imagine it so,
Just beyond where the wild rose grows.

IV
It was her
A wild rose
[Her sanctuary]

The mud brick house,
On the Rim, a caboose,
Payson's octagonal abode.

These places were sacred
For the feelings they created
& where her love flowed.

Pine needle floor,
Under the trees,
There was her shelter.

Sun porch decor,
She would sit in the breeze,
Mockingbird, her protector.

To feel your presence, or imagine it so,
Just beyond where the wild rose grows.

V
It was she
A wild rose
[Her obituary]

Jane always said
Her ashes should be spread
Over the edge of the abyss.

To the sound of the chorus
Beyond the edge of the forest
Where the wild rose is.

Oh to have had
Just one day more,
One day more with you.

To hold your hand
As we stood at the door,
Before you had to go through.

To hear your laugh, or imagine it so,
Just beyond where the wild rose grows.

MOTHER MOON - REMIX

WILD ROSE

Mother Moon gazes out
    From her celestial
    Sewing room
Across a turquoise sky.

                              A vision of my dream.

One, among the devout,
    Carries a glass vessel,
    To the tomb
& sings her lullaby.

                              The faint sound, recorded.

Appearing through the clouds,
    A divine parallel,
    Calling forth
Grace, with her peaceful sigh.

                              Image, captured on film.

Remembering the moon
    We gather together
    As we mourn
& as we say goodbye.

                              Teardrop in the ocean.

CROSSING OVER & BACK AGAIN

WILD ROSE

A white torch of light
Cast off our distant sun,
Piercing an expansive sky,
Punching through the glass,
Crossing the room,
& striking the bare skin
On the back of my hand.

Freckles turning
The color of dried blood.
Small hairs catching fire
In shards of light & heat.

Then there is the soft & gentle caress,
A brush across the edge of my wrist
A warm reassurance of your presence.

Crossing over from beyond,
Your touch pushes reality aside
Causing an incendiary lapse of reason.

Your journey from the other side
Crossing the stage,
A finger on the source,
Orchestrating a pit of fury,
A rage of pain, and sorrow.

SUSPICIONS

WILD ROSE

You must have known
Those nights you came home,
You must have had suspicions.

You must have known he was being disloyal.
With menthol butts in the dirt
The scent of perfume on his shirt
& the open brandy tucked behind the Crown Royal.

You must have had suspicions.

I wonder now if you were as mad at me,
as you were at him in the end,
When you found out
We all knew that he had a girlfriend.

You must have known I knew.
You must have known we all knew,

& when you found out it would have been
As if your entire family betrayed you.

You must have known.
You must have had suspicions.

SCATHING INQUIRY

WILD ROSE

Singing fingers on piano keys, playing,
Dancing as raindrops begin to fall.

Her apron is draping, knives are a-scraping
Her scissors chasing a paper doll.

Drawing the lace curtain open, to the side
Revealing a rich carnal delight.

Raking soft marrow from the bone, we decide,
To stay safe in the kitchen tonight.

A SILENT PRAYER IN THE NIGHT

WILD ROSE

Standing in the dark forest clearing
I hear a cry in the night air
Fearing for what this sad song will bring
I turn inward, saying a prayer

When instantly the sky turns to stone
A symbol of divinity
Staying silent, I think I'm alone
Yet souls count to infinity

Blessing her life with soft bells to toll
A faint light leads me towards the day
I propose a toast to lift her soul
Hoping angels will show the way

RESILIENT

WILD ROSE

Touchstone: A memory pushing me forward.

Intense is her nature
Squaring off against
A limitless ocean of adversity,
Brandishing a gentle posture
Defiant & resolved.

Planted as deep as a stalwart oak
Gripping a well-worn cane
Not to lean against, but rooted,
Pressed into the hard soil
As if to slow earth's churn.

A descendant from a determined tribe
As adamant as the fabled lodestone,
[Antiquity's measure of strength, captured]
Who held their heads high.

An oak does not drop leaves because
It grows tired of carrying them.
It drops them because
It doesn't need them anymore.

A THIMBLE FULL OF SEEDS

A dram of abundance.
Potential renewed,
Oh! To live again!

Defining the afterlife.

A spirit among living,
An apparition moving within
Two states of being.

Not quite separate from life,
Crossing between
What we know as life & death.

Consider a seed:
Potential renewed,
Life after death.

Entombed in a dead husk,
Then released into the world,
To rejoin the living.

This Spirit created in life lives on beyond life itself.
Death carries forward its promise.

A thimble full of seeds:
Hope for distant renewal & life again,
Among the desert grasses.

CHAPTER 9

DEATH OF ART | ART OF DEATH

The changes to her cognitive state were obvious; every time I visited her a little more of who she was had slipped away. The memories we had shared were becoming my memories only.

After she had been hospitalized, her mental state changed even more. Prior to that point she had been sad & forgetful, but afterwards she seemed to be frightened & distraught. Nothing seemed to calm her agitations.

The reality was that each time there was a change in her physical space, her cognitive abilities suffered a further setback. There had been moments when she remembered things & people, but most of the time she couldn't recognize our faces or communicate.

Watching her struggle with her reduced mental state was deeply saddening. The normal joys she had in living were replaced with fear.

Art was life for her. It was how she saw & interacted with the world around her. It was both her language & her lifeline. She saw art in everything that surrounded her.

Her art lives on, an expression of her love, speaking to us through our pain.

B. EUGENE B.

God created a brilliant tableau
With a nut-brown acorn
& the cast-off feather from a crow.

Interpret new meaning from old proof
Telling stories anew
Hoping to find evidence of truth

In like manner, in a river's flow,
Silt drifts in the current
Making ethereal art below.

She had always connected through art,
But memories dissolved,
Grew into shadows, & broke her heart.

The dementia grew like a broad thread,
Where, deeply embedded,
Art dies; creativity is dead.

WILD ROSE

ASHES

WILD ROSE

Released into the wind,
Carried over the ledge,

At a place where I want to kneel down.
Where I want to curl up & hide.

A place, someday,
To leave my body on a grate
(& bid the crows to eat).

So I can be carried away
Under the wing & into the sky.

My spirit welcomes release there
In the place where they reside.

WHAT IT MEANS TO MOURN

WILD ROSE

Collected together
Bluntly aware
Knowing her death means
Different things
To each of us.

Alone in our loss,
Behind sheets of tears.
Connected by memories.

Though one in grief,
We are far off in sad thoughts.

Touching the quilt she made,
Holding a spoon she used to stir the pot,
Finding a card she wrote remind us,
That these small memories
Keep her alive.

But we keep to our grief
For now.

MOM'S EYES

WILD ROSE

Your eyes, your gaze
In your dying were so soft & so distant
Compared to the piercing stare
I remember when we were both younger.

Your younger brown eyes
Could see right through me
Could see around corners
& in the dark
Could see me no matter what.

Your eyes could be loving
& then filled with motherly concern
In an instant.

You could see my thoughts with those eyes

But time stole away those eyes
& age stole away their glimmer
& you saw new things in a new way.

But in the days before you passed,
Your eyes pulled spirits
To fill the spaces, still.

In the form of an owl alive -
Looking down from above -
Come to take your spirit.
Come to be your eyes.

PERHAPS TOMORROW

Perhaps tomorrow I will feel less
pain
Perhaps tomorrow I will feel happiness
again
Perhaps I will be able to smile
At the sunshine
Perhaps I will be able to smile
When it rains.

I have been told that someday
When time has passed,
That I will look back
& smile at memories
I have of our time together
Of you
& joy will again fill my heart.

But I hope to always remember
The pain I feel now
As a testament of what you have meant to me.

MORNING IN THE MOUNTAINS

If ever there is closure
I won't stop remembering
The images of your creation.

The knick knacks,
With painted faces, flowers, & bugs,
& watermelon wedges from logging cuts.

Closure is a softening of the pain,
Not an end to it.
An awareness that what has passed is removed forever
From a future potential
Into a gentle place called memory.

Which the smell of rose potpourri
Will activate again & again.

THE LAST DAYS ON EARTH

WILD ROSE

The last days
On earth.
The last hours
Of life.
The last breath & then passing.
Leaving before tomorrow's parade.

Living & then living no more
Dying & resting in peace.
Superseding the ocean in blueness.
A vast panorama of love.

Stones worn smooth by running water
Adorning their arms & legs.
Green & yellow garlands
Worn on their heads & necks.

Watching the sand & silt slip between your fingers.
As it was,
Holding your hand,
Telling you stories,
Hoping you could remember.
Hoping you could join me in joy
I will see you on the other side.

The morning slipped by
I was too overwhelmed to cry
Except when I tried to describe
To others that you had died

I was your youngest son.
You gave me life
& now I hold your head against my cheek & I cry

DEATH WATCH

WILD ROSE

Oh, wooden owl on the wall,
Staring as she crosses over & is released.
Carved eyes softly watching all,
Sole witness to her crossing to eternal peace.

The wooden eyes there to see
The sad moment of her soul lifting up
& passing into the sky, taking her place among distant stars.

Looking beyond this present breath
Find it in yourself to bless each one.
Many, tonight & every night, think death
Is a disguise, a sentimental shard we become.

But death is something deeper than that
Deeper than what we can ever believe
Death is forever becoming
Coming from a place up God's immeasurable sleeve.

Where owls watch over the dead
& the dead watch over us.

SAY A LITTLE PRAYER

Lord thanks, Amen.

B. EUGENE B.

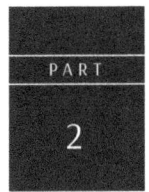

OTHER POEMS SUNG BY THE WINDOW

THE WORLD WE KNOW IS NOT REAL

WILD ROSE

Running through the meadow,
Hear the ladybugs sneeze?

Listening to the bark
Talk back to the trees.

Cupping hands to catch shadows
Falling from the leaves.

Luckily I'm not an aphid
I am hopeful you would agree.

COLLECTING ROCKS

WILD ROSE

Tearing through skin on the back of her leg,
Pebbles relentlessly caressing the sun,
The flint blade rests beside a pool of blood.

Cutting holes through a careless, sparse, & subtle bubble;
Getting ready to burst onto the surface,
Shamelessly splattering mud.

Send ripples through her face,
[The clearest molten glass].
Bend stone into curved shapes
To fit the surrounding noises.

We gather carefully to share
An immaculate palette.
The world awaits the burden of our bounty.
Scalding & false, a reduction.

Not fallen but leaning forward
Towards the light & walking two-by-two
Forward from the back of her face.

The pace of changelessness
At the peak of the subtle heat
Collecting rocks, shimmering,
In life's expected outline.

CHASED BY CHANGING WINDS

WILD ROSE

The soft wind comes at last,
Wakening the grass & trees.
It follows me as I try to hide,
But I will never outrun the breeze.

I discover as I push through
A hollow where fallen angels have been,
(Amongst bramble & wild grape vines)
A fearful place, this burrow of sin.

The wind comes up again behind me,
It must surely know my way.
No matter how fast or far I run
On my heels it seems to stay.

It is then I feel distant eyes are watching
Demons waiting for me to trip & fall
I hear murmurs of their hateful plans
& feel the terror in their evil call.

These angry ghosts want to bestow
Their collection of evil from old.
I mustn't let them find me alone
Or else they'll snatch me into their fold.

So thus the wind becomes my fair companion
Granting me safety in the sky.
I must believe I am blessed because
The wind tells me I shall not die.

WINDOW DRESSING

WILD ROSE

The canvas-top wagon has become my home
In a caravan along an endless path.
It's a slow pilgrimage which we are now on
Fool's errand, we all forgot how to laugh.

We stopped where the toadstools gather at the edge,
I secretly hoped I would have found you there.
In a house of unhewn stone without windows,
Amongst brambles & briars of despair.

Finally we're setting our souls to go free,
(Significance in the timing of release).
Freedom, but at the far edge of a sharp cliff,
Between pebbles & a steep precipice.

Now stretch your soft flanks out against the smooth rocks,
Soak long in the depth of absolute stillness.
Watch as columns of steam rise from the soft stone,
Warming your blood to clear mental illness.

Blue smiling lips make shapes instead of words,
Like the silhouettes of jagged floral shapes.
With spiraling stems & sharp curlicue leaves,
But despite all, nary a breath escapes.

DESERT MIRAGE

WILD ROSE

    The lone road crosses a dusty field & leads up to a house tucked under the meager shade of an old palo verde tree. A place where shimmers of heat soften the edges of the horizon & where dust devil plays havoc with the small dog running alongside, trying to bite at it.

Savory scene
Where saltbush grows thick
On the lip of the ditch.

Where grapevines grow,
Stretched on trellises
& clothes hang out to dry.

An angry shed
Where lashes are dealt,
Hiding from light of day.

Where people go
To eke out their means
Of life & where they die.

While the mountains beyond,
Bear witness to it all.

NEW CLOTHES

WILD ROSE

Planting of trees to hide behind,
Yet scary eyes see through the boughs.
Stay solid; I pray that this night,
I might somehow survive their throes.

Follow the spot behind your eyes,
Watching for the sun as it grows.
Seeking the curved madrone trunk,
A fine spot for counting crows.

Dripping in light from underneath.
Scaring my friends, scaring my foes.
Just then it explodes on my lap,
Ruining all my nice new clothes.

SECRET PLACES IN THE FOREST

WILD ROSE

Opening up in front of us, a long winding path,
The round unnamed meadow lies waiting.
With black-eyed Susans circled around
A small water hole in the center that stays
Dry all summer long.

Larson Canyon, the meadow we knew as Long Tom,
With a sheep-herder lookout & gnarled cave
Formed between giant boulders leaning together, side-by-side,
Beside a deep pool in the rocks
Where salamanders lost their gills
& grew legs every summer.

Christmas Tree Canyon,
Far back St. Joe's Road,
Where I always felt I was being watched.
By living beasts
& restless spirits
The hair on my arms assured me it was true.

The outline of log cabin homesteads,
On the road where we found diamonds in the creek,
Only their foundations left as a reminder
Of the people who once arrived here
Thinking this was where they belonged.

Wildcat Canyon, a narrow place,
Where the road crossed the wash by the salt lick
Where Mom collected wedges
Cut & left by loggers
& painted them to look like watermelon slices
& rocks she painted with a parade of blue ladybugs
With eyelashes.

ONE FOR THE ROAD

WILD ROSE

The train soundly slipping forward in the rain,
It's what a home-wrecker's dreams are about.
Having true devotion to suffering & pain,
The endless loop of a homeward bound route.

Hellfire inside his reckless brain,
The radio buzzing like it's about to explode,
The windshield wipers slapping away in vain.
Crashing down the winding road.

Beer & whisky sloshing in his gut
The road washed out by the flood
The tires slide and spin out in the rut.
With each turn more booze enters his blood

The crossing gate, the red lights flash
His Chevy tries to make up for his lack of skill
But it can't beat the train & buckles in the crash
Too fast to notice as he comes down the hill

DENSE HEADSPACE

WILD ROSE

Out of sync with the cycle of stars
Particular to this evening
Dense headspace pulling random thoughts
Slowly across the ceiling.

In my deranged mental morass,
I meditate to calm my monkey mind.
But unsettled thoughts somersault,
& screech as they climb up my spine.

Small idea for a larger calling
Depleted chance to begin dreaming
So give me peace & allow me rest
Instead of dragging me, kicking & screaming.

Just as the sun begins to rise
I slip gently into the land of dreams
But sleep here is not so deep
With sunlight slipping between the seams.

BUOYANCY RESERVED FROM A PAST LIFE

WILD ROSE

You must forgive me
In the forever that is now.
For what transpired in lives passed by
For breaking a solemn vow.

A paper bag with scraps at the bottom,
Life torn from the pages of scarce memory,
Folded dreams become the alibi
& proof it wasn't treachery.

The scant residual proof of our reunion
A testament to a past life as one,
What chance do we have, you & I,
To make a life again circling around the sun?

What will our life be like from now on?
You must forgive me, please, somehow.
Come & join me in the sky,
In the forever that is now.

CHAPTER 29

FIRE

WILD ROSE

Dry grass praying,
Asking to become,
The conflagration.
Just waiting for the spark.

Fire & wind to burnish the prairie.

Yellow straw, crisp grain, tall thin stems,
Carry the fire forward
Into the field
Not as an encumbrance
But as a joy to behold.

Heat & smoke rising in a broad column,
Creating a shimmering shadow across the edge of the road.

The firestorm creating its own infamy
For our remembrance.

AIR

WILD ROSE

Blank space chock full of air.
Fear not this descent to hell,
Instead be confident amid despair.
An empty void, a vacant shell.

Oh, what was yours before.
When time stopped God's exhale,
& shut the future, as if a door.
Scarce remnants left on death's scale.

WATER

Sacred water balloon-faced god
Streaming out her mouth,
A trail of arrows.
Powerfully cowering placidly beside some inner turmoil.

Join with a simmering taboo,
Selling hubcaps & doing a slap-happy dance.
Mimes (cropped at the top) in the powdered snow,
Boundlessly silent behind the curtain.

Cancer grows forward across the lungs
Pushing out & closing in (the space between)
Forcing gasping breaths that don't support the life within.

Water spills across the front
Splashes & fills the gaps
Suck in the brown river.

Washed eyes to keep small
Pupils from wandering
Inside | outside | the desert air.

I can't make it without you
Thundering bottom rung
From here to Tumacacori
& back again.

OVERTURE

WILD ROSE

A start of something substantial:
Tangible
& yet
(Unfortunately)
Quickly
Forgotten.

[Then we left the broken door
& savored the small bitter herb.]

Turned sideways
We could barely be seen.

   Turned inside out
   We'd certainly make a scene.

      Turned on a spit
      They'd serve up our spleen.

         Turned into marmalade
         We'd form a thick sticky sheen.

Sadly it was our last meal &
The first time we'd eaten in days.

MOVEMENT

Inadequately aligned,
A sticky situation triggers fear.
Causing instability in orbit,
& collision with other spheres.

  A primordial solution is emitted
  When we face existential problems
     (Elemental - delicate & yet discarded)

  Forming the basis
  Of our survival plan.

Blessings sprinkled down,
Given from something divine.
Given as small precious gifts,
Leaving no trace of origin behind.

Carry no token into the temple
Lowered eyes but standing tall.
Come in low & be gentle,
Resist letting out your caterwaul.

Often described as soft spoken,
Like gentle waves on the ocean,
Or a chain reaction unbroken
Within the mechanism of motion.

A GASPING

WILD ROSE

Breathing through a mask,
Gasping for a breath of fresh air.
Try to stay on task,
Staying safe in a world of despair.

I do what I can to stay well,
Contained & socially distant.
It's hard to catch my breath in hell.
Without being persistent.

Wearing a mask, an N ninety-five,
I try to avoid making a scene,
Hoping I can somehow stay alive,
In the time of COVID-nineteen.

SOUP

WILD ROSE

In this scary world our coping strategy
Is often unable to resolve what we fear.
It seems that in the history of our anatomy,
An anti-anxiety organ has failed to appear.

It is in this world that we evolve,
This gastro–intestinal soup of our lives,
Where hair & claws quickly dissolve,
& yet the plastic we create survives.

So as I say farewell to my bones & teeth,
I say farewell to the rules to which I abide.
Farewell to my prior religious belief,
Welcome to the creed to which I now subscribe.

MOTHER-MOM-MOMMY-MOMMA

WILD ROSE

Mi Madre applauds your crossing-over
Arriving in a field of rye grass & clover
Up from the depths of the river in which you drowned
Smelling of medical-strength soap
You come to the surface in a hospital gown
Still holding on to that old tangled rope
Which held you down.

Deep inside had been the fear you would fail.
But therein also lies the promise.
Was it your ability? Was it your inability? Which would prevail?
Would you find uncertainty? Or would you find solace?

Depressed, alone, & all but certain
That day, you wished it might never come
There was nothing left, except your pain.
You didn't feel it, you were too numb.

Slowly begin to understand;
It's was a long road, without a doubt,
Built upon a foundation of sand
One way in, & no way out.

CHAPTER 37

A GATHERING (UNDER THE SUN)

WILD ROSE

We take the time to come,
We take the time to gather.
Find each other, in our time,
Come to speak of the matter.

With ancestors held close,
In memory, they remain.
Spirits mingle in this place,
We come together again.

Come to speak, come to learn,
Come to gather their wisdom,
Come kindle fires which burn,
Come let us ignite the sun.

SONGS OF BEUREN (OH! I GOT MONEY PROBLEMS)

WILD ROSE

How I howl,
& scream,
& cry!
Injustice follows me
Wherever I go.
I can't catch a break.

When I sing my sadness goes away,
Oh! So I sing even more,
Songs lift the veil of pain,
& I feel more blessed than I did before.

But still, how can I earn money
If all I ever do is sing?
Am I doomed to suffer alone,
Do I want to know what tomorrow may bring?

The songs may be written & unsung
Hidden in a stack of clutter
But tonight I glory at the stars
From my bed here in the gutter.

DERBY DAYS

WILD ROSE

Memory: life in the necropolis,
Standing alone, hesitant to explore.

Dreaming now, as the river moves past me,
The last river in the world anymore.

Coming to know the truth about her death,
Catching shadows which were unseen before.

It carries me back to the days of old,
When the burning pyres lit the skies in gold.

Orange-yellow sun touches the face of earth,
The only sun this world cannot ignore.

THE REIGN OF THE OCTOPUS QUEEN

Now drifting under the ocean,
Visions of the refracting light.

Conveying rippled impressions
With songs of aquatic delight.

Spinning through spiny crevices
Approaching great depths, still floating.

Feelings carried from distant shores
Grow until they are exploding.

Carried ashore by breaking waves
My mind overflowed with wonder.

In my arms an empty basket
Which had once been filled with water.

THE MOON CARRIES ME TONIGHT

WILD ROSE

Silently she climbs, emerging below,
Passing in front as she begins to rise,
Luminously adorned, she casts her glow,
Joining together, we fill the night skies.

The silent stars stay still, waiting for us,
Yet we refuse the urge to surrender,
In this, a vast expanse of endlessness,
We'll journey as companions together.

She will shepherd us on our path this night,
Her soft tears sink & swell in broad oceans,
Embers uplift and, like stars, they delight,
As we dance in slow circular motions.

& thus we consecrate this sacred place,
Spirits summoned across all time & space.

B. EUGENE B.

ABOUT THE POEMS CONTAINED HEREIN

CHAPTER 43

ABOUT: WILD ROSE

Wild Rose is the ode to the poet's mother. The imagery in this poem comes directly from her long life, including such details as the mud (adobe) house and the caboose where the family lived in the mountains. Written within days of her passing, the poem speaks in raw emotions & is guided by her loving influence on the poet's life. A complicated relationship, that of mother & child; additionally, the poem reveals deeply held beliefs about what life after death means to those who are still living. The precipice dividing the two souls is impossible to span & so the pain of the loss is compounded with the pain of realizing it as such.

Mother Moon - Remix traces the poet's imaginary dreams after the death of his mother. Her artwork (with sun, moon, and floral motifs) had a great influence on his perspective. The image of her in her workshop, staring down from the stars above, carries forward this effect.

Crossing Over & Back Again records a paranormal visit after death; the first whispering of a presence beyond the living. The topic of past lives and the soul's journey in the afterlife is a recurring theme of the poet. The emotional response to the situation (rage) is driven by profound grief and the disconcerting effects of lost reason due to underlying mental health issues. The inspiring imagery is drawn from memories of sunlight on hands at the dinner table during family gatherings; many hands coming together in prayer & then holding utensils to carve the meat.

Suspicions is the first time the poet has tried to process his father's infidelity, and the whole family's complacency, from his mother's perspective.

Scathing Inquiry records visions from the poet's childhood, images of his mother.

A Silent Prayer in the Night is a meditation on the process of trying to accept death, in the form of a dream.

Resilient describes mom's years living alone in Payson, Arizona. It is set in relation to the elements that sustained her spirit beyond time - the ocean, the earth, & the trees.

A Thimble Full of Seeds Consider the seed, a tiny spawn from the dried grass stem discarded to the wind. It is more powerful than any of us reading this poem. Stand in awe.

Death of Art | Art of Death is a rumination on remembrance, a study of the mind's frail nature, & the poet's worst nightmares made real.

Ashes is a song of wishes, to be at Sheep's Creek Point again & forever.

What it Means to Mourn is a reflection on the family gathering, after mother's passing, to spread her & father's ashes. The memorial, at the family retreat in the mountains of northeastern Arizona, was an opportunity to reflect and rediscover threads of meaning from their parents' life together, and to pass on stories to the next generation of family members.

Mom's Eyes is a poem about the last days spent with mother, at her bedside, as she stared with her eyes scarcely open. Her eyes were his eyes - they were indistinguishable from each others'. Eyes tell the story behind the storyteller's lies.

Perhaps Tomorrow moves from the pain of loss through the rationalization of loss & eventually to the knowledge that, though loss is forever, our feelings are always changing. It reflects the anxious grasping at current feelings, not wanting to lose that pain even if other things change.

Morning in the Mountains is set on the Mogollon Rim (what we called "up in the mountains"), with the season of beetle demise, then the desert near the Doll-Baby Ranch, at the base of the Mazatzal Mountains, & ends back in the wispy land of rebirth.

Closure recounts how, in the first weeks & months following a profound loss, small reminders bring tears to the surface. It is important to understand that we remember "things" about a person as we process our overall emotional memories that are identified with them, but in the totality of it, we experience these things as if they were remnants; parts left behind.

The Last Days on Earth is the raw emotional memory of the soft, smooth skin of his mothers forehead against his cheek as he kissed her goodbye.

Death Watch is about the small wooden owl, a gift sent to mom, which the nurse coincidentally hung on the wall directly in front of her deathbed.

Say a Little Prayer is the prayer mom first taught us to say when we couldn't remember the longer prayer said at dinner time. The longer prayer, which the older kids and adults said, was, "Lord, I do give thee thanks for the abundance that is mine, amen."

ABOUT: OTHER POEMS SUNG BY THE WINDOW

The World We Know is Not Real - blends the fairy tale of the surreal with our reality (a thin line indeed). The danger of living in either state is pure bliss. Need I say more?

Collecting Rocks is cloaked as a tribute to a favorite pastime of searching for magic rocks but is alarmingly set against a dark & solemn ritual of death.

Chased by Changing Winds follows the trajectory of a sweet dream as it turns evil. The moment when a clear restful sleep becomes shrouded with the demons stretching out their hand.

Window Dressing is a vision of what life would have been like in a different place & a different time.

Desert Mirage is a recollection of memories from driving across the desert and passing lonely houses that were miles from any other structures & wondering what happens behind those closed doors. Still a mystery & will always be, but not an unexamined mystery. Ditch dry, day, die, all.

New Clothes is a transect study of forms of life inside the mind, a mind teetering between the state of mental illness & stillness. A dream journal's delight.

Secret Places in the Forest explores a few of the magical places in the Sitgreaves National Forest in northeastern Arizona. These stanzas explore the past while touching the present & stretching to the future. These places, if not already named, were often given names by my Mom for features she noticed there.

One for the Road recounts a mix of actual memories & imagined nightmares in a rush of blind stupidity.

Dense Headspace describes the place that poetry became in my darkest hours. The cadence & purpose of poetry provided a structure to my mental wanderings, making sacred the morning & evening ritual of spiraling down into my grief, my longing.

This work of poetry became a very dense headspace for me. It was a place where poetic ideation in my mind was ordered by a strict internal protocol of structure and tone.

It was a thick place where I spent time weaving in & out of a prescribed pattern, a guide or template which over-layed the thoughts of my mind. In a thick & elaborate blanket of impressions, these deep kaleidoscopic images formed & reformed from segments of memories & from my overly active imagination. It was a predestined spillover from my nightmares which I am unable to shake in my waking hours. It is where I lived. It was my reality.

Buoyancy Reserved from a Past Life speaks to the pain of love lost.

Fire doesn't allow you to escape unscathed. Sacred to the Zoroastrian, I come to fire with caution and respect. The burning in my heart is the fire of passion consumed.

Air covers the earth, is it the exhale of God? Can the plants save us from our own exhale?

Water is the source of life on earth & in a ritual of renewal washes down on us, through us, and back into the earth. Life grows, diseases grow, the eyeball rotates (rolls) in its socket, all kept in motion because of the water we seek to stay alive.

Overture is what happens to our mortal bodies when we don't find time to spread joy in our lives.

Movement calls out the jagged edges of motion that intrude on the rituals of rest & inactivity.

Gasp for Air was inspired by the day the poet first tested positive for *Coronavirus Disease 2019*, after three years of successfully avoiding it. The idea had always been to wear a mask to keep the virus out but suddenly he had to make sure his mask kept the virus contained.

Soup traces back the existential threats we face to the disruption in the microflora of our guts caused by a military-industrial complex fed on American cheese and white bread. The question of whether we can survive depends on our ability to return to the diets which nourish the body, mind, and spirit.

Mother-Mom-Mommy-Momma strikes fear which rises from the earliest memories of maternal presence surrounding the child, until the end.

A Gathering (Under the Sun) follows the cadence of a fire burning hot in the hearth, of a hot sun burning the earth.

Songs of Beuren (oh! I got money problems) is the personal soundtrack of Carmina Burana, interpreted through a personal lens, not a theatrical production. In fact, it is only playing in my head.

Derby Days is a vision of a cinematic dream sequence, sunlight filtered through the smoke & dust, with the ancient city like a mountain on the horizon and the funeral pyres rising like sharp fingernails clawing their way from under the earth.

The Reign of the Octopus Queen is an aquatic vision of a cinematic dream sequence set not in a necropolis, but in the realm of the deep ocean.

The Moon Carries Me Tonight is an incantation of earth & moon in divine embrace. Written as a sonnet (three quatrains and a couplet).

AFTERWORD

There is no way I could ever willfully stop the creative process - it is as much a part of me as is the blood that fills my heart. I can't hide the frenetic energy which is in my mind & spins off in various forms of artistic expression. Nor would I want to hide it. The process of creation is what defines me.

While "In a Past Life & Other Poems Sung by the Window" was a tribute to my dad, "Wild Rose & Other Poems Sung by the Window" is an ode to my mom, Jane Marie, who passed away on April 6, 2022, at the age of 86.

"Wild Rose" is a collection of poems drawn from memories of her life & from my feelings of loss & of mourning her passing. It has been a painful time for our family but we are blessed with many beautiful memories of her life; through these memories her spirit continues to bless us from afar.

The title comes from the wild roses she grew from rose hips which she collected in the forest near our cabin on the Mogollon Rim, in northeastern Arizona. She loved roses in general but those wild roses in particular. My favorite photograph of her, from my nephew David & included in her obituary, shows her sitting on the porch of the cabin next to these roses.

Mom was an amazingly creative person. Always filling the world with her art, she had a distinct style that imprinted on my mind from the earliest ages. She painted floral motifs in the corners of the windows of our home, portraits of all of us (as suns) on the dining room chairs, & even the bottom of our pool one year (with an octopus & fish).

It really is no wonder that I can't stop creating art - it is literally in the blood that fills my heart. & this book is meant to be an ode to her, a picture book in words to capture the love she gave to the world.

www.ingramcontent.com/pod-product-compliance
Lightning Source LLC
LaVergne TN
LVHW012028060526
838201LV00061B/4507